I0555140

The CBCT® for
Business and Leadership

Implementation Guide

Bringing Compassion Training
into Organizations

Center for Contemplative
Science and Compassion-Based Ethics
Emory University

Contents

Introduction

The volatile, uncertain, complex, and ambiguous (VUCA) world we live in requires individuals, leaders, and organizations to have resilience and the ability to cope under pressure. Compassion is uniquely placed to support this ambition. Despite global challenges, a number of organizations are adopting a more human-centered, compassionate approach to business and leadership and aligning their strategies with the world's wider sustainability and wellbeing needs.

This guide offers a strategic methodology for implementing such a compassionate approach, as well as practical information for organizations and business leaders who are keen to develop such an approach. Whether seeking to adopt compassionate practices throughout the employee life-cycle or supporting employee wellbeing, CBCT® (Cognitively Based Compassion Training) is an effective, research-based program that delivers tangible results in participant wellbeing, resilience, and engagement.

With the aim of supporting organizations as they enhance and sustain wellbeing in their communities, this guide provides a structure for delivering a systematic and sustainable culture of organizational compassion. This structure includes a step-by-step approach for implementing CBCT for Business and Leadership into an organization. CBCT for Business and Leadership works in partnership with existing organizational structures and is designed to complement the expertise and programs within an organization to improve leadership and organizational outcomes.

The implementation process outlined here is designed for business leaders, change management and HR professionals, leadership and development teams, and other stakeholders involved in setting a business's culture and direction, as well as delivering overall change. Each organization is unique, and so CBCT for Business and Leadership can be tailored by those implementing it to meet the specific needs and ambitions of their communities.

Through the development of a considered and well-constructed approach, alongside a commitment over time to delivery, CBCT for Business and Leadership can be implemented in a manner that contributes to the wellbeing of all stakeholders and employees and improves organizational culture, effectiveness, and outcomes.

"Compassion is essential for survival. Without cooperation, trust, gratitude, and reciprocity—as well as the many other qualities associated with compassion—humans would not have survived, let alone flourished."

— Dacher Keltner, *Born to Be Good: The Science of a Meaningful Life*, 2009

Program Overview

CBCT was developed by Emory University's Center for Contemplative Science and Compassion-Based Ethics (colloquially, the Compassion Center). CBCT is one of the first research-based programs to study the physiological, psychological, and behavioral outcomes of compassion training. It is one of the most researched compassion training programs available today, and it demonstrates an impressive array of measurable benefits for participants' wellbeing.

A growing body of research links compassion training to greater individual resilience and wellbeing. Studies have repeatedly demonstrated that compassion training not only lowers stress hormones and strengthens immune response, but also decreases rumination, activates pleasure circuits in the brain, increases self-reported happiness, fosters more optimistic and supportive communication styles, and serves as an antidote to burnout.

CBCT has been specifically adapted for particular audiences, such as physicians and other healthcare providers, educators, and, now, those involved in business and leadership. CBCT offers this latter group an important resource, as it is uniquely placed to offer practical, evidence-based approaches that can lower individual stress, improve resilience, and decrease the likelihood of burnout. Moreover, studies have shown that the relational reserves created by such compassionate approaches are strongly correlated with positive organizational outcomes, including employee engagement and improved wellbeing, and even organizational survival.[1]

In 2004, CBCT was developed by Professor Lobsang Tenzin Negi, bringing together complementary tools from the Indo-Tibetan Buddhist tradition and the emerging science of emotions from psychology and biology, to develop an educational program that contributes to human flourishing. CBCT is a secular program that walks participants through a set of contemplative practices and helps them establish and cultivate

CBCT Research Outcomes

Significant decreases in:

- stress biomarkers and inflammatory response[2]
- depression[3]
- loneliness[4]
- PTSD symptoms[5]

Significant increases in:

- hopefulness[6]
- compassion and related neural activity[7]
- empathy and related neural activity[8]
- self-compassion[9]

For published research on the above outcomes, visit *compassion.emory.edu*.

26
Countries Represented
by Teachers

15
Languages

300+
Certified Teachers

15
Certified Senior
Teachers

6,000+
Full Course
Participants

15
Introduced
to CBCT

a readily accessible sense of safety, develop greater self-awareness and emotional pliability, and increase compassion for the self and others.

As of 2024, CBCT has certified over 300 CBCT teachers from 26 countries, who are teaching CBCT in 15 languages. CBCT has been offered to over 6000 participants from diverse populations in research settings and to the general public via courses at Emory University.

How Does CBCT Stand Out From Other Programs?

▶ CBCT holds the distinction of being one of the longest-running and most studied compassion protocols of its kind.

▶ CBCT is linked to improvements in health and wellbeing across studies.

▶ Rather than a one-size-fits-all approach, CBCT has been tailored to various sectors, including education, healthcare, business, and for mental health practitioners, by experts in their respective fields—all with impressive results.

▶ CBCT forms the cornerstone of a strategic global initiative, the Compassion Shift®, which aims to advance a global culture of compassion.

Learn more about the Compassion Shift initiative at: *compassionshift.emory.edu.*

CBCT for Business and Leadership

In 2024, Emory's Compassion Center launched this uniquely tailored program—CBCT for Business and Leadership—for those who work in organizational settings. CBCT for Business and Leadership is a compassion training program specifically aimed at enhancing resilience, compassion, and overall wellbeing for leaders and employees, as well as building skills associated with social and emotional learning. It is designed to include practices that support a greater sense of wellbeing, empowerment, efficacy, and connection to people as they move through their work and personal lives.

For many years now, CBCT training has had a transformative impact on business leaders, HR professionals, healthcare providers, military veterans with post-traumatic stress disorder, parents of children with autism, transgender youth and their parents, breast cancer survivors, hospital chaplains, and many others. Although the needs of some of these groups might seem distant from those of the business world, it is worth remembering that many work colleagues are also parents, carers, and survivors.

CBCT is neither a management fad nor a theoretical academic model. Instead, it is a practical, sustainable means of delivering individual and organizational wellbeing. The early adopters of CBCT in business are already reporting positive results. Organizations across a variety of sectors—including healthcare, education, consumer goods, supply chains, legal, and non-governmental—are realizing the significant individual and organizational benefits of embedding CBCT into their workplace cultures. As CBCT continues to expand its global reach, these results are within reach of all organizations, regardless of their size, location, or the challenges they face.

Whether an employee or otherwise, people suffer in myriad ways, both inside and outside of work. As well as the human cost of such suffering, the World Health Organization[10] estimates that $1 trillion per

Learn More About CBCT for Business and Leadership

Training Compassion for Business and Leadership: The Official Guide to CBCT® for Business and Leadership (2025).

Compassion U™, the digital learning platform for all CBCT courses. For more information about the CBCT program, courses, and how to bring it to your organization, please visit: *compassionu.app*

"Managing compassionately is not just a better way to build a team, it's a better way to build a company."

— Jeff Weiner, CEO, LinkedIn

CBCT in Business Early Adopter Testimonial

"To paint a picture of where I was before CBCT – well, 'anxious' can probably sum it up. Every incident, no matter how minor it was, felt like a mountain in mind. I suffered depressive episodes often that affected my personal relationships and the quality of my work. The mismanagement of my emotions throughout a stressful day would leave me completely burned out. I was on the brink of walking away from my job.

During the course, I was exposed to a different mindset, a new way of looking at myself and the world. To experience an environment of calmness was like a comfort food (but without the negative consequences). The time I spent doing the CBCT practices added solace to my day, insights into problem solving with compassion, and, most importantly, self care. What some people saw as my hard exterior gave way to a softer, gentler, more connected human being who is kinder to myself and others. Socially, I'm mindful of my reactions versus my responses. I have a more embodied understanding of how deeply connected we are to one another, and how much we rely on each other."

annum is lost in the global economy each year through depression and anxiety and their associated productivity loss. Moreover, approximately 15 percent of working-age adults were estimated to have a mental disorder in 2019, and this has likely increased since the pandemic. However it is measured, suffering is costly, and so compassion matters.

In CBCT for Business and Leadership, participants learn a variety of methods to deliberately strengthen the crucial skill of resilience, using self-reflection exercises to better manage the ups and downs they face, both professionally and personally. Through activities and practice, they deepen their emotional awareness and self-compassion and, in doing so, uncover and unlearn habits that may be hindering their sense of well-being. Participants then focus on connecting with others, both close to them and distant, to develop tools for managing challenges and emotions, and to deepen their compassion for others. As participants apply the skills learned in their CBCT practice in the workplace, the organization becomes more compassionate and resilient. In this way, CBCT for Business and Leadership provides a whole-systems approach to organizational wellness and culture change, as well as significantly contributing to participants' wellbeing.

Business leaders' personal practice of CBCT also brings about subtle (and sometimes not-so-subtle) changes in their emotional and social intelligence. CBCT practices are designed to shift small interactions—use of language, tone of voice, or gestures—that can make a world of difference to individual colleagues and, from there, to organizations as a whole. These shifts may not all be conscious to the leader or others, but neuroscience tells us that we can pick up on these subtle signals even unconsciously, and they can shape our levels of trust and confidence with each other. As a strong sense of psychological safety grows in the organization, the organization's resilience, wellbeing, and professional outcomes all benefit. The disproportionate impact of leadership's behaviors and emotion on employee wellbeing and results is well documented. As leaders reinforce these essential practices for their organizations, they are simultaneously improving their own wellbeing and efficacy, as well as positively impacting organizational outcomes.

"The thing that makes us love our jobs is not the work that we are doing, it's the way we feel when we go there. We feel safe; we feel protected; we feel that someone wants us to achieve more and is giving us the opportunity to prove to them and to ourselves that we can do that. And by the way, it's good for innovation, it's good for progress, and it's good for profit."

— Simon Sinek, author of *Start With Why and Leaders East and West*

Implementation Process

A cohesive plan for implementing CBCT for Business and Leadership in organizations goes beyond offering one training or workshop. Sustainable implementation involves a thoughtful approach to bringing CBCT to each organization in a way that meets its specific needs and allows for opportunities for the approach to be integrated in culturally meaningful ways.

The Four Components
of CBCT for Business and Leadership Implementation

1	Set the Foundation	Lay the groundwork, engage the senior team, allocate resources, align with existing organizational vision and structures.
2	Engage the Organization	Introduce CBCT for Business and Leadership to the organization and develop plans for implementation.
3	Implement the Training	Deliver CBCT for Business and Leadership training.
4	Support Ongoing Integration	Sustain, develop, and continuously integrate CBCT for Business and Leadership.

CBCT for Business and Leadership aims to develop competencies in resilience, awareness, discernment, and compassion, which will then contribute to the wider organization's culture of compassion. CBCT is also designed to enhance the wellbeing of employees, leaders and other stakeholders by reducing physical and emotional symptoms of burnout, increasing employee retention and engagement, and improving individual and organizational outcomes. Embedding CBCT for Business and Leadership into an organization allows for better conflict resolution and can improve employees' creativity and collaboration.

Organizations must manage finite resources while investing in their employees' development and wellbeing. By implementing CBCT, each organization can significantly impact the outcomes of individual employees and the context within which they operate. Investing in the wellbeing of all employees is to invest in the resilience and outcomes of the organization. This section outlines various options for how organizations can implement CBCT into their systems at varying scales and across multiple sites or geographical regions.

Sample Three-Year Path: Implementing CBCT for Business and Leadership

0–9 months
Set the Foundation

- Engage in exploration of CBCT for Business and Leadership.
- Cultivate buy-in among senior leadership team.
- Establish focus groups around wellbeing / CBCT to assess the need and to consider whether CBCT or another resource is right for the organization.
- Establish baseline measures and determine how these interact with other established, cultural aspects, (e.g., pulse surveys / employee engagement surveys, feedback mechanisms).

9–15 months
Engage the Organization

- Build organizational capacity to implement CBCT for Business and Leadership.
- Establish strong communications, training, and stakeholder engagement plans prior to wide-spread implementation.
- Establish stakeholder and steering groups, with orientation session to ensure openness of selection process across organization.

15–21 months
Implement the Traning

- Pilot Training Compassion for Business and Leadership course.
- Assess pilot results and gain feedback to inform wider rollout.
- Implement the training for existing and new employees, at all levels of seniority.
- Measure results.

21–24+ months
Support Ongoing Integration

- Engage and adapt to ongoing integration.
- This stage is about moving from project implementation to a compassionate-business-as-usual phase.
- Refresher training for existing employees and training for new employees should be offered.
- Support further practice.
- Integrate into employee lifecycle.
- A regular cadence of updates and successes to be incorporated into the wider organizational communication plans.
- Longitudinal measurement.

Component 1
Set the Foundation

1 **Set the Foundation** Lay the groundwork, engage the senior team, allocate resources, and align with existing organizational vision and structures.		**Determine Roles and Responsibilities**
		Consider Needs and Readiness
		Establish Aligned Goals and Vision

Determine Roles and Responsibilities

There are three key organizational groups required in the implementation of CBCT, each with specific responsibilities: (1) the senior leadership, (2) the steering group, and (3) the implementation team. As in any change initiative, considering who is best placed in each of these roles, and ensuring everyone is clear on responsibilities, is crucial. At the outset, these groups will likely be made up of those members of the organization who are familiar with CBCT and have already bought into the value of implementing the program. These groups should be established in this early phase. Each group might start out with only a few members, and some members may take part in multiple groups at once. The process for creating and expanding these groups will depend on each organization.

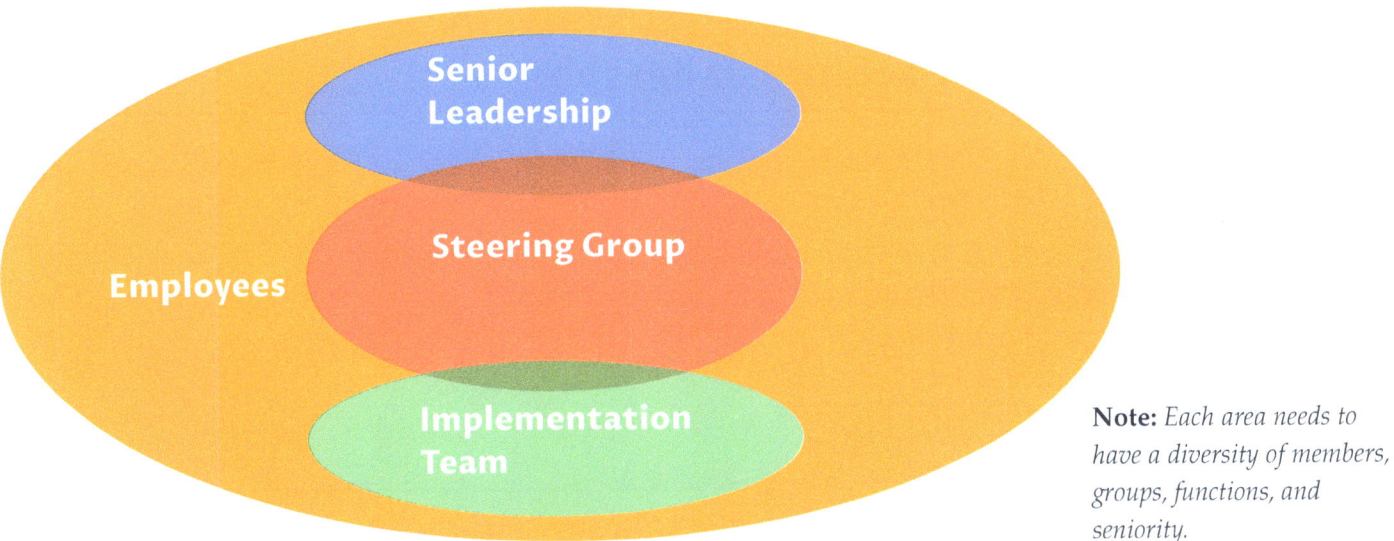

Note: *Each area needs to have a diversity of members, groups, functions, and seniority.*

Senior Leadership

Leadership's disproportionate impact on an organization's overall functioning and wellbeing is well documented. This is true whether the leadership focuses on delivering shareholder return, improving operational efficiency, or introducing change initiatives. In any situation, the role of leadership is to communicate a clear and compelling vision, prioritize resources to deliver this, and model the desired organizational behaviors. Research in organizational psychology emphasizes the importance of leadership at all levels to "view compassion as part of organizational culture and legitimize and propagate it."[11]

It is, therefore, unsurprising that the role of leadership in an organization is critical for the successful implementation of CBCT for Business and Leadership. Leaders should authentically embody and model CBCT principles, and clearly support their implementation. In doing this, senior leadership can successfully support CBCT's integration into the organization's cultural fabric.

For effective implementation in any organization, CBCT needs to be sponsored and supported by the senior leadership. Initially, this may be driven by one individual (e.g., the CEO, HR director, or other C-level role), or by a group of individuals keen to engage in this work. The exact size and nature of the leadership supporting CBCT implementation may vary over time, and will likely adapt as needed in response to internal and external factors. The role of the senior leadership will be to establish goals and vision with the implementation team, allocate resources, receive and approve proposals, agree on baseline and ongoing measures, and model desired behaviors.

The Role of Senior Leadership

Model commitment to implementation.

- Actively engage in the training.

- Apply CBCT for Business and Leadership skills and perspectives to enhance personal wellbeing, support more helpful and meaningful interactions with others, and better manage and inform tasks at work.

- Adapt CBCT skills to suit specific organizational challenges.

- Integrate CBCT for Business and Leadership principles and practices into daily tasks and responsibilities.

- Incorporate practices into organizational cadence and meeting structures.

- Ensure principles are incorporated into policies and practices across the organization and throughout the employee lifecycle.

- Establish consistent and clear messaging of CBCT concepts and topics across direct, small-group, and whole-group communication.

Manage sponsorship and engagement.

- Introduce CBCT to the organization, and continue to be an active, visible sponsor of the approach.

- Introduce the training to the organization, and ensure sufficient time and other resources are allocated to enable this to happen effectively.

- Visibly participate and engage in the training.

- Communicate about the benefits and importance of implementation (regularly and consistently, formally and informally), sharing personal experiences where appropriate and useful.

- Share early successes to build momentum and address any inertia or cynicism.

- Celebrate the accomplishments of individual colleagues, teams, and the wider organization as they engage in CBCT for Business and Leadership.

Establish organizational systems and structures, and allocate resources.

- Establish a CBCT steering group that can support implementation and ensure appropriate adaptation to changing circumstances when needed.

- Allocate the necessary support and resources (financial, operational, human, and others) to provide time and space for staff workshops, training, and practice.

- Develop CBCT-specific objectives and targets for individuals and teams to align desired practices with organizational outcomes.

14

Steering Group

The steering group is composed of some of the senior leadership and some members of the implementation team. Its role is to provide support and offer constructive criticism to the implementation team; ensure the readiness of proposals presented to senior leadership; and ensure a wide range of employee views are included. The role of the steering group can vary depending on the context, scale, and culture of the organization.

Note: *The steering group is widened in Component 2 to include more employee representation.*

The Role of the Steering Group

Support the implementation process.

- Support the pilot of Training Compassion for Business and Leadership with a small group of change implementers.
- Establish a community of practice.
- Develop and encourage a mentoring program.
- Ensure that a diversity of opinions and a wide range of input mechanics are available to all employees.

Explore and develop expertise in the CBCT concepts and practices.

- Engage in CBCT practices and reflections as a team.
- Reflect on personal and professional growth.

Review and evaluate the results of the Training Compassion for Business and Leadership pilot.

- Identify the strengths of the pilot, and develop creative solutions to address any barriers or challenges.
- Use pilot data to inform the the widespread rollout of CBCT for Business and Leadership.

Oversee the implementation team.

- Ensure deliverables remain on track and budgets are met.
- Assess the clarity and efficacy of communication.
- Manage motivation.

Implementation Team

The implementation team works with the steering group to support the implementation process. Some members of the implementation team may also be members of the steering group. The role of the implementation team is to execute the key elements of the implementation process—to deliver the trainings, ensure measurements are completed, and report progress to senior leadership.

The Role of the Implementation Team

Report implementation progress to senior leadership.

Deliver communications, stakeholder, and training plans.

Run the pilot and subsequent wider rollout (with support from the steering group).

Ensure readiness audits and course assessments are completed and reported.

Consider Needs and Readiness

No two organizations are the same, and so it is important to conduct a needs assessment and readiness audit before launching CBCT for Business and Leadership in any specific context. Indeed, for multi-site or similarly complex organizations, multiple such assessments may need to take place to ensure appropriate tailoring.

Through an auditing process, the implementation team will be able to advise on the current organizational climate and conditions for implementation, including capacity, resources, assets, and needs. Readiness for change and change-fatigue assessments are also important areas of consideration, which can be read in conjunction with existing organizational structures, such as employee wellbeing surveys. The results of these audits inform senior leadership decisions regarding CBCT training options, implementation structures, and areas for particular focus.

As the implementation team designs the optimal needs assessment and readiness audit for their organization, some particular areas might be useful for consideration (and for steering group discussion), highlighted in the following questions.

Guiding Questions – Consider Needs and Readiness

Describe the overall staff morale. What would support, improve, and/or sustain the current culture and climate? What is working well, and where are areas of concern?

What is already in place (wellness programming, health initiatives, team-building activities, staff appreciation events, etc.) that you can build upon and use to support this work?

What is the composition (seniority, skill levels, geographical reach, etc.) of your employees and other stakeholders? What service duration patterns are there? Is there high staff turnover, or do employees tend to stay for a number of years?

When (if ever) do you offer professional development time, and how can this time best be used to meet employee and organizational needs?

What financial, human, and physical resources do you already have, and how can these best be utilized to plan and support the training and implementation of CBCT?

What does your organization have the capacity to commit to? What will be needed to sustain the work of CBCT implementation?

Are there groups or individuals you can identify as potential early adopters of CBCT for Business and Leadership (individuals who may already be interested or would be more likely to express interest)?

Who are your disproportionate influencers? Are there any skeptics or detractors who would benefit from additional focus?

What external resources (speakers, peer organizations, CBCT teachers and materials, etc.) are available?

 ## Establish Aligned Goals and Vision

An important step for the successful delivery of CBCT for Business and Leadership is for the organizational senior leadership to understand their role, agree on a vision and goals for the work, and allocate appropriate resources to the implementation. Broadly, the senior leadership must consider how to align CBCT to the organization's existing goals and vision, position CBCT alongside established or emerging initiatives, and clarify how CBCT can deliver on existing strategic plans.

Senior leadership should consider the following questions before implementing CBCT for Business and Leadership. Through thoughtful consideration of these questions, combined with the outputs of the needs and readiness audits, the leadership team will be able to articulate the main goals of implementation and put together a brief description of the vision for CBCT in their organization.

Guiding Questions – Establish Aligned Goals and Vision

What are the main goals and desired outcomes of implementing CBCT for Business and Leadership in this organization? Can you identify specific changes that implementation would lead to in the organization?

Are there particular needs or issues that must be addressed in the organization?

How might CBCT for Business and Leadership help address the needs of the organization?

CBCT is evidence-based and has a significant body of research that demonstrates its reliability and validity across many geographical and organizational settings. How can CBCT be integrated into existing employee wellbeing offerings and/or institutional structures to support individual and organizational flourishing?

How does the implementation of CBCT for Business and Leadership fit into the existing organizational vision? How does this work align with the existing values and culture?

Component 2
Engage the Organization

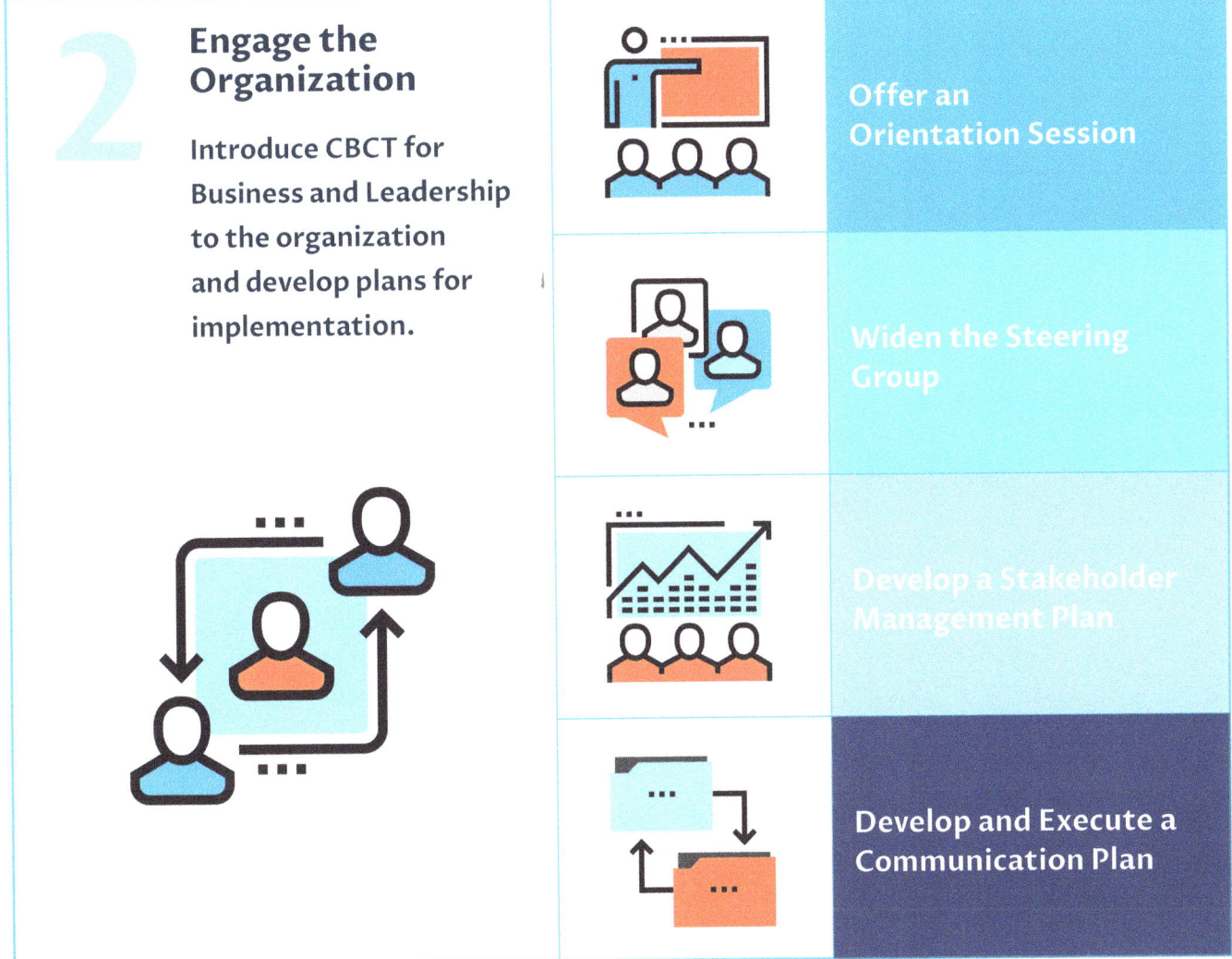

Engage the Organization

Introduce CBCT for Business and Leadership to the organization and develop plans for implementation.

Offer an Orientation Session

Widen the Steering Group

Develop a Stakeholder Management Plan

Develop and Execute a Communication Plan

Once the needs assessment and readiness audit have informed a strong business case, and senior leadership has signed it off, fuller employee engagement can begin. This is important, as people should not have CBCT "done to them"; rather, individuals should be supported to make an informed choice about their next steps with CBCT.

 # Offer an Orientation Session

The orientation session aims to introduce CBCT for Business and Leadership to members of the organization who can serve as the program's early adopters and/or those who would be interested in being involved in the wider change process. The leadership should determine who from the organization will be invited, as well as the size and frequency of orientation sessions; there is no one correct way to do this, as it will depend on each organization's culture and circumstances.

This orientation session lasts one to two hours and is designed to provide employees with a basic knowledge and understanding of the CBCT for Business and Leadership program; to outline the program's overall design; and to describe how the program can be implemented.

This session can be facilitated by senior leadership or a member of the steering of the group. When introducing CBCT for Business and Leadership to employees, it is important to communicate thoughtful and carefully crafted messages that align with the wider organizational vision and culture. The facilitator of this session should be authentic and model desired compassionate behaviors when communicating with employees. An example orientation structure is provided in the following section.

Orientation Session Content

An Overview of CBCT for Business and Leadership (~15 min)

This section will briefly outline the framework and background of CBCT, its benefits for participants, its approach to cultivating resilience and wellbeing, and the science that supports it.

The Implementation Process (~30 min)

This section goes over the organizational goals of implementation. Ideally, it should be shown how these align with the outcomes of the readiness audit. This section should also outline next steps, timings, and employee engagement possibilities, such as joining the CBCT steering group or participating in the training. When describing the implementation process, the facilitator should:

- Articulate a clear alignment to existing organizational vision and strategy.
- Articulate a clear rationale for choosing to implement CBCT for Business and Leadership.
- Be authentic about your personal investment in CBCT for Business and Leadership.
- Make connections between CBCT for Business and Leadership and other wellbeing initiatives that might already be part of the organizational culture.
- Highlight how CBCT stands out. What makes CBCT different? Discuss the challenges and opportunities that may arise from this work.
- Acknowledge, if appropriate, the possibility of change fatigue in the organization.

Discussion, Collaboration, and Further Communication (~15 min)

Lastly, the facilitator should field questions and hear from session participants about ideas, areas for further consideration, and any concerns. In preparation for this discussion, the facilitator will lead the group in the co-creation of guiding principles that will make them feel safe, heard, not judged, etc.

The content and outcomes of the orientation session can be made available to the whole organization via communication channels, as appropriate.

Note: *For a more in-depth overview that includes reflective and interactive practices, a certified CBCT teacher is required to facilitate the session. See "Introductory Offerings" on page 28 for more information.*

 # Widen the Steering Group

Note: *This is also an opportunity to invite stakeholders to join the implementation team. Refer to pages 15–16 for more information on the different roles of these groups.*

Once CBCT for Business and Leadership is introduced through the orientation session, different members of the organization may become interested in engaging in the implementation work. This is a great opportunity to invite colleagues to join the CBCT steering group.

Developing and maintaining a CBCT steering group helps the implementation process to be inclusive and creates opportunities for members of the organization to participate in the process. This group allows employees from different departments, levels, and even geographies to be involved in the implementation and feel a sense of ownership over the work.

The make-up of a CBCT steering group will vary based on each organization's values, structure, capacity, and ambition. The steering group's composition depends on the organization's size, purpose, and function. It is beneficial to have a senior person with decision-making power as an active part of the group. The team should be collaborative, with representation from as many stakeholder groups as possible.

CBCT Implementation across Multiple Sites

The approach taken to successfully implement CBCT for Business and Leadership in one location may not be the same for implementing at another, even within the same region. Therefore, training staff and implementing CBCT for Business and Leadership may require some site-specific adaptation.

If you are scaling CBCT across multiple sites, the recommendation is to work through the process at each site, specifically. Determining readiness factors is a good place to start when developing the process and approach to CBCT implementation. This approach will support each site in utilizing current systems, structures, and personnel most effectively for a successful implementation.

When implementing CBCT for Business and Leadership across multiple sites, it is ideal to form a central CBCT cross-site steering group with representation from each site. This group can have similar goals to the CBCT steering group and can use their time together to share concerns and ideas and support each other. The team can also align methods (such as data measurement tools, measuring outcomes, communication and messaging plans, community events, etc.) to support consistency.

 # Develop a Stakeholder Management Plan

The implementation team should deliver the stakeholder management plan in conjunction with the wider steering group to receive sufficient feedback and guidance prior to submitting the plans for senior leadership's approval.

Conduct a Stakeholder Audit

In Component 1: Set the Foundation, the implementation team conducted a readiness audit (see page 17), which can inform a stakeholder audit. If useful, a broader network of organizational stakeholders can also be approached and asked to participate. While optional, repeating this process can be beneficial, as it allows the organization to better understand stakeholders' perspectives, thus supporting CBCT's successful implementation.

Develop Stakeholder Plan

Using input from the audit, use stakeholder mapping tools to identify stakeholder risks and opportunities, and then develop a detailed relationship management plan to address these. This plan will require clear prioritization of areas to address and should be strongly linked to the overall communications plan. Listening to and engaging with stakeholders is the responsibility of both the implementation team and the steering group.

Monitor and Adjust Stakeholder Plan as Needed

Stakeholder engagement can be monitored through a variety of methods, depending on which is most suitable for the organization. Interviews, surveys, focus groups, and feedback are all useful methods. The implementation team and steering group should review the outputs of these methods and adjust their stakeholder relationship management accordingly.

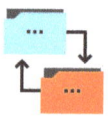

Develop and Execute a Communication Plan

The CBCT steering group and implementation team should work together to develop a communication plan. The purpose of communication related to CBCT for Business and Leadership is to inform and engage employees about why CBCT is being implemented, what they can expect from CBCT, and how they can get involved in CBCT.

Communication Plan Goals

▶ Gaining support from organization employees

▶ Sparking interest in different stakeholder groups

▶ Developing relationships to allow for questions and exploration of CBCT

▶ Sharing information about different CBCT offerings and practices

▶ Keeping people engaged and excited about CBCT practices and training experiences

▶ Providing support for initial and ongoing CBCT integration

Component 3
Implement the Training

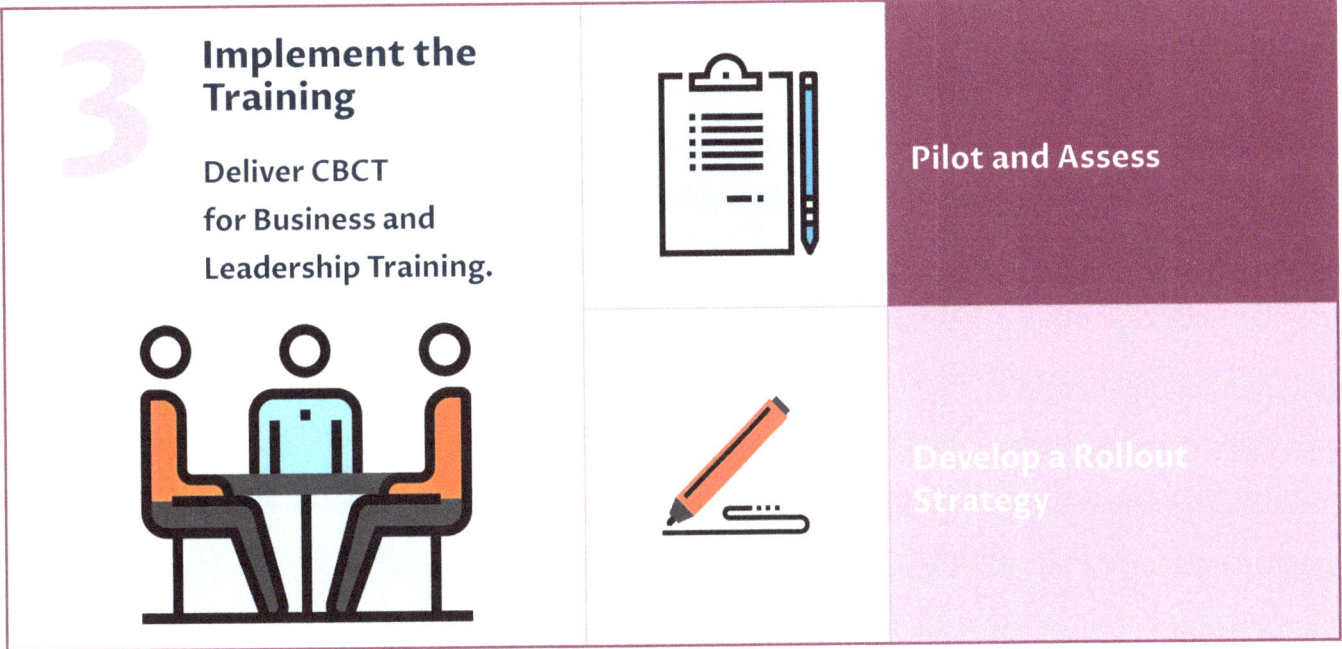

Implement the Training

Deliver CBCT for Business and Leadership Training.

Pilot and Assess

Develop a Rollout Strategy

Pilot and Assess

Training Compassion for Business and Leadership is the full CBCT for Business and Leadership course. This course involves moving through a sequence of 10 self-guided learning experiences: Overview, Modules 1–8, and What's Next. The eight modules of CBCT each strengthen a particular skill or insight, and the modules build on each other to foster greater resilience and compassion.

Training Compassion for Business and Leadership (16–24 hours)

Brief Description: A deep dive into the eight CBCT modules, tailored for those who work in organizations. Each module introduces new content, reflective exercises, and practices designed to strengthen inner skills and insights and support their application into everyday life.

The Training Compassion for Business and Leadership course is offered through Compassion U, a user-friendly app that delivers CBCT course content and provides access to instructional videos, activities, practices, and a compassion community, among other resources.

Courses include live sessions with other participants, facilitated by certified CBCT teachers. These live sessions are typically one hour each and occur weekly over nine weeks. Prior to each live session, participants engage in the self-guided content, activities, and practices on Compassion U.

This course can also serve as a prerequisite for those who are interested in applying for the CBCT Teacher Certification program.

Format:

▶ Self-guided on digital learning platform, Compassion U (8–16 hours, typically 1.5 hours per week)

▶ Live sessions in person or via videoconference, facilitated by a certified CBCT teacher (9 hours of live sessions, typically 1 hour per week)

Piloting Training Compassion for Business and Leadership

When possible, running a pilot of the Training Compassion for Business and Leadership course allows each organization to gain additional data and insight into its specific needs. A pilot enables assumptions to be tested and interest to be gauged before starting a full implementation. The results can also provide useful success stories that may be useful for the full implementation of CBCT for Business and Leadership.

When planning to pilot the course, consider the following steps:

- Select or develop surveys to administer pre- and post-pilot to assess the impact of the course.

- Identify the early adopters who you want to pilot the course with.

- Find an Emory-certified CBCT teacher who can lead the live sessions for the course.

- Determine the format of the training (meeting frequency, length of sessions, online or in-person, etc.).

- Identify the date(s) and time(s) the pilot will take place.

- Enroll the early adopters into the pilot course.

- Make sure those enrolled have access to Compassion U (which houses their self-guided content and practice resources).

- Administer surveys pre- and post-pilot. To protect privacy and encourage honest feedback, we encourage you to ensure the personal data collected is anonymous and secure.

 ## Develop a Rollout Strategy

The path for CBCT for Business and Leadership training will vary, depending on the organization's specific needs and structure. The senior leadership should decide the timelines and the balance of compulsory versus optional CBCT enrollment. The CBCT steering group, in conjuction with the senior leadership and implementation team, can evaluate the results of the pilot and determine the best approach to offer the training to their employees and other stakeholders. This should include options of in-person versus online and the timeframe for delivery of each training.

When developing a rollout strategy for CBCT for Business and Leadership, consider the following steps:

Want to Bring CBCT to Your Organization?

Visit *compassionu. app/ for-organizations*

1 Determine which group(s) you are bringing CBCT for Business and Leadership to.

2 For each group, determine which offering makes the most sense to start with (the full course or one of the introductory offerings—see the following section for more information on introductory offerings).

3 Choose an Emory-certified CBCT teacher to facilitate the experience.

4 Determine the format of the training (meeting frequency, length of sessions, online or in-person, etc.).

5 Identify the date(s) and time(s) the training will take place.

Introductory Offerings

In some cases, members of the organization may benefit from an introductory experience to give them a sense of the content and practices of CBCT before beginning the full course. This section details several of the introductory offerings.

Overview of Training Compassion for Business and Leadership (30 minutes–1.5 hours)

Brief Description: The Overview offered in the Training Compassion for Business and Leadership course on Compassion U is an Overview. This self-guided experience orients participants to the content and practices of the course, introduces compassion and compassion training, and includes reflective exercises and practices that set a foundation for the course and give a glimpse into the types of experiences that participants will engage in throughout the rest of the course. The Overview is a free experience available to anyone through Compassion U.

Format: Fully self-guided on digital learning platform, Compassion U

Introduction to CBCT – Seminar (45 minutes–3 hours)

Brief Description: An introduction to CBCT, including a sample practice or two. This training provides an overview of CBCT, including an exploration of the framework and history, its benefits for employees and leaders, its approach to cultivating resilience and wellbeing, and the science that supports it.

Format: Live session in person or via videoconference, facilitated by a certified CBCT teacher

A Taste of CBCT – Workshop (4–8 hours)

Brief Description: This workshop exposes participants to the key themes, skills, and insights of the CBCT course, and introduces some of the reflective exercises and informal and formal practices. This workshop provides a taste of the CBCT experience, allowing individuals to begin exploring and strengthening the capacities related to resilience and compassion before diving into the training. This could be done in one long session or broken up into several shorter sessions over multiple days.

Format: Live session(s) in person or via videoconference, facilitated by a certified CBCT teacher

Component 4
Support Ongoing Integration

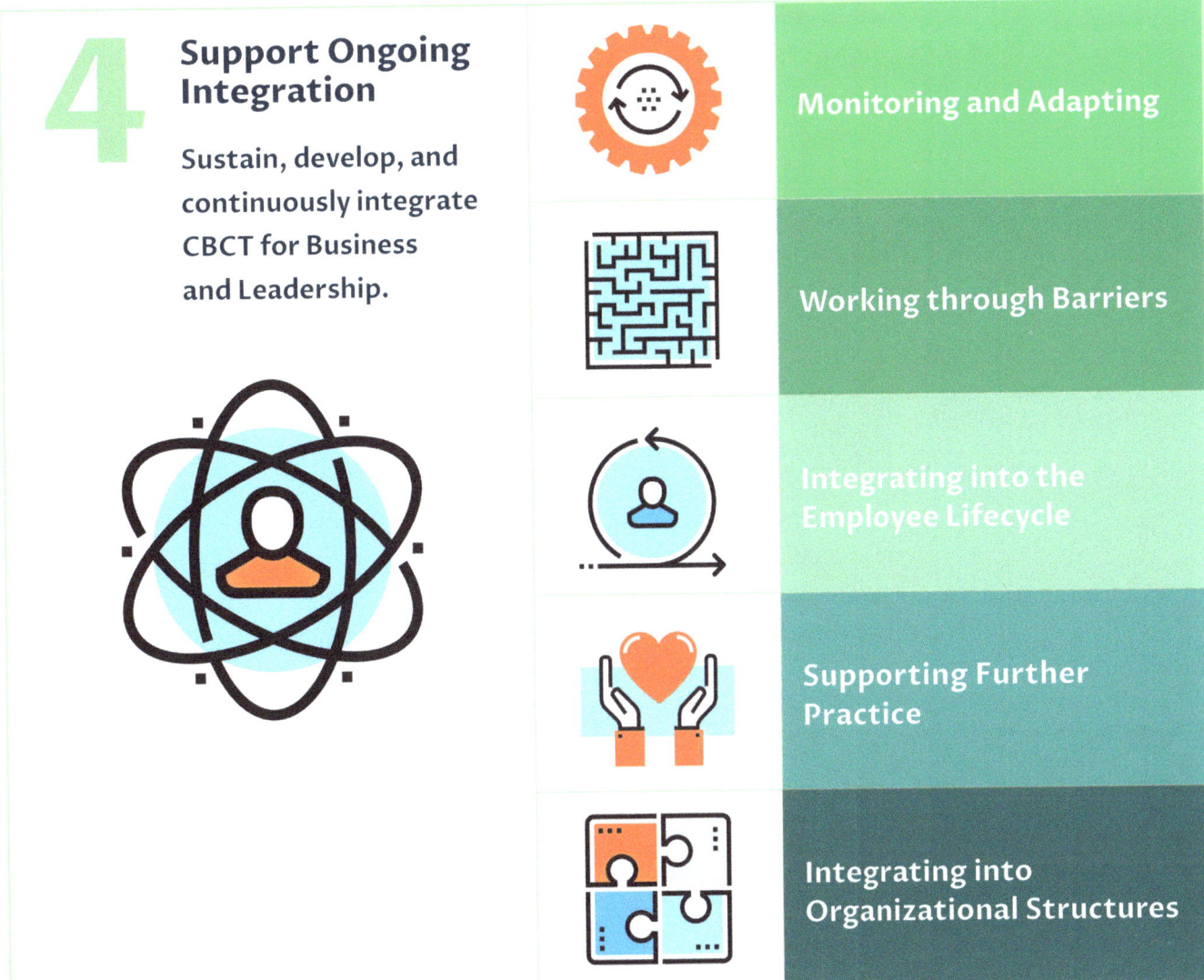

4 Support Ongoing Integration

Sustain, develop, and continuously integrate CBCT for Business and Leadership.

- Monitoring and Adapting
- Working through Barriers
- Integrating into the Employee Lifecycle
- Supporting Further Practice
- Integrating into Organizational Structures

No two organizations are the same, and so every organization's CBCT implementation will have its own challenges, complexity, and nuances. The five areas outlined in this section allow for successful ongoing integration.

Monitoring and Adapting

Implementing and integrating CBCT for Business and Leadership requires regular and consistent reflective practice. Feedback on how the program is being received is essential for the program's success and for maintaining employee buy-in. Maintaining an understanding of how the program is resonating with employees and stakeholders relies on ongoing monitoring. Feedback can come in the form of written feedback, formal and informal conversations, and observations. Each of these forms of feedback provides leadership with a unique and important insight into the impact that CBCT for Business and Leadership is having on employees.

On the basis of the feedback, recommendations to adapt and improve the implementation can be developed. This may mean providing additional training, enhancing communication, or even developing new integration strategies for CBCT practices and related activities.

Working through Barriers

Implementing any new initiative will inevitably encounter some barriers and challenges. Identifying and addressing these is key to continuing and sustaining meaningful work over time. Supporting the ongoing integration of CBCT occurs through the regular effort to celebrate, engage, and train employees in CBCT for Business and Leadership.

Time

▶ There is inevitably pressure on time in any organization. Prioritization, visible senior support, and long-term planning are key to finding the time for CBCT training. Another successful way to address the issue of time is to deliver the training in bite-sized periods of time; facilitating a 10-minute presentation can lead to interest in a 1-hour session, which may then lead to a half day workshop.

Money

▶ All organizations have finite financial resources and must allocate these accordingly. The cost of CBCT is relatively low and is best viewed as an investment in the wellbeing of employees and the organization more widely.

Buy-in

- Many organizations have effectively implemented CBCT for Business and Leadership by first offering training to those who show an active interest, even if they make up a very small group. Once this group reports on their experiences and shares the benefits of the training with others in the community, the implementation can build on this initial success.

- Buy-in is also directly related to an effective communication plan. Helping the organization to understand the benefits and value-add proposition for them personally and professionally is critical. Reflecting back the experience and feedback from CBCT participants within the organization will go a long way in building credibility, fostering authentic engagement, and promoting overall buy-in.

Communication issues

- Change initiatives often falter because the organization fails to provide consistent and ongoing communication about a prioritized initiative. Through multiple forms and iterations of communication, it is critical for senior leaders to voice and message the impact, benefits, and progression of CBCT integration and training throughout the organization.

Competing needs

- Many initiatives exist within every organization. CBCT for Business and Leadership's ability to be overtly linked and aligned with the overall organizational strategy and subsequent initiatives is critical for the success of the overall implementation.

Leadership and staff transition

- Leadership and staff turnover are inevitable in any organization. Establishing a culture and climate characterized by resilience, awareness, and compassion will ensure that the transition of key employees does not undermine efforts to further CBCT for Business and Leadership training and integration.

 # Integrating into Employee Lifecycle

Integrating CBCT into the employee lifecycle will support its transition from a change project to a sustainably integrated approach to "business as usual." One of the surest ways to embed CBCT is to ensure it is relevant at every part of the employee lifecycle.

The following was reprinted with permission from Papworth, K.D. [2023] *Compassionate Leadership: For Individual and Organisational Change*. Berlin: De Gruyter Brill, 156–158.

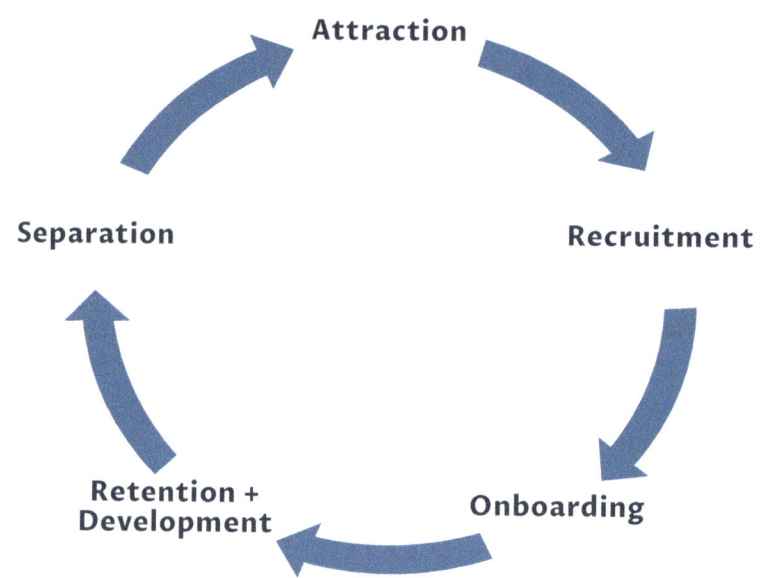

During job design, advertising and recruitment, the compassionate aims of the organisation can be stated, roles can include explicit responsibility for the wellbeing of self and others, and candidates who are unsuccessful can be treated with dignity. Time is precious, yet giving feedback to such candidates may make a significant difference to the disappointed individual, as well as reflecting well on the organisation.

For appointed candidates on-boarding is a crucial time to set a compassionate tone and expectations, as well as for the organisation to hear fresh perspectives and ideas. During my . . . research interviews, one of the respondents commented favourably on the post-hire policy within his organisation. This included conversations each quarter for the first year with HR, focusing on his opinions about the organisation, any area he was struggling with and offering suggestions for improvements. Becoming aware of issues in this structured way was a first step towards compassion and change.

Personal development is . . . an important precursor for [employee engagement]. Such development can include formalised compassion training, as explored later in this chapter, both for line managers and others. In organisations where such interventions take place, [employee engagement] levels increase and employees often report that . . . [compassion training] and common language around compassion make potentially difficult conversations easier to handle.

If we want to retain employees, we need to notice when they are struggling or disengaged at work. Compassionate leaders can support individuals, understand underlying issues and simultaneously notice repeating patterns. Formal structures for support, for escalation and even for whistleblowing all provide necessary signposts that lead to compassionate action and employee retention.

Varying circumstances of departure from an organisation, whether voluntary or not, positive or otherwise, will necessitate different approaches. Even a difficult exit is best treated with compassion, as both the person leaving and those staying all fare better when departures are handled well. Exit interviews—alongside more proactive 'stay interviews'—are useful. Beginnings and endings require close attendance, so when an employee is leaving an organisation, whether through their own volition or otherwise, taking the time to hear their concerns is a useful individual and organisational investment. Compassion is a commercial approach even at this stage in the employee lifecycle, as engaged, positive organisational alumni can be a useful source of future talent, recommendation and opportunity.

Within the employee lifecycle, compassionate leave is increasingly common in organisations, and can be a useful 'catch all' policy for a myriad of situations. The need to recognise and address suffering has recently resulted in the introduction of compassionate policies covering shared parental leave, adoptions and miscarriages. Previously taboo subjects such as the physical and psychological impacts of the menopause have yet to become mainstream policies, but the tide is moving in that direction. If this suite of policies feels too difficult, too costly or too time consuming for an organisation, it is worth remembering the research which demonstrates that people who feel compassionately cared for in a time of need will generally recover more quickly (Post 2011). Furthermore, they will likely return with a renewed and improved sense of engagement and positive inclination towards the compassionate organisation. As noted by one of the participants in my . . . research: 'Compassion can get people through issues more quickly, so it's a commercial decision to be compassionate.'

Hiring and Onboarding Staff through the Lens of Compassion

When hiring new staff, develop interview questions that specifically gauge a candidate's familiarity and fluency with practices related to CBCT (including emotional regulation, decision-making, and care for others). For example:

- Can you tell us about a time when you supported a colleague who was working through a challenge?

- Tell us about a time when a customer or peer had differing views on a project. How did you respond to this situation?

When onboarding new staff, CBCT for Business and Leadership can be introduced in the new-staff orientation and through mentorship:

- **Orientation:** The orientation is a great opportunity to introduce CBCT and begin to engage in the practices. This is an opportunity for the organization to prioritize and highlight the culture of compassion they are working to embed.

- **Mentorship:** Under the guidance of skilled mentors with a high level of CBCT knowledge, new staff can better understand and benefit from the culture of compassion and feel motivated to engage in the initiative or learn more about it.

Annual Appraisal and Feedback with a CBCT Focus

With employees having been primed to concepts and practices such as cognitive reappraisal, self-compassion, and other CBCT for Business and Leadership–related topics, their integration can occur within the annual feedback and evaluation process. Providing opportunities for reflection and self-evaluation in a manner that is related to CBCT could look like the following:

- How have I grown in my ability to handle adversity, conflict, and stress?

- What strategies to foster resilience do I apply when dealing with difficult situations or navigating conflict?

- How am I using different CBCT practices to enhance my awareness, resilience, and compassion for myself and others?

- What tools or strategies do I use to reappraise different situations?

- How has CBCT for Business and Leadership supported my wellbeing?

- What are ways that I want to continue to foster personal wellbeing and resilience?

 ## Supporting Further Practice

Some employees may wish to sustain and deepen their practice beyond the initial training. The organization can support this by encouraging individual practice, encouraging group practice, and certifying employees in CBCT.

Encouraging Individual Practice

While often done in group settings, the CBCT for Business and Leadership practices are personal practices aimed at strengthening a participant's inner skills and capacities. This inner work is not complete in 1, 5 or even 100 courses, but rather is understood as a lifelong practice—something we all continue to engage in, train, and apply throughout our lives. Finding the time and space to engage in the practices and incorporate them into our busy schedules and existing routines can be challenging.

Encouraging and supporting this practice amongst your employee community can make it more likely for participants to continue engaging in the practices and can make them feel supported, nourished, and motivated. Consider the following ways to encourage individual practice:

✓ Create a space for relaxation and contemplative practice

✓ Integrate CBCT practice within the existing employee wellness and health offerings

✓ Establish a community of practice for interested members of the organization

✓ Provide subscriptions to Compassion U for interested employees

Encouraging Group Practice

Communities of practice

While individual groups may choose to form their own communities of practice, the organization should offer more structured offerings. These groups can meet regularly to:

▶ **Debrief the modules in sequence:** Go through the modules again together, taking time on their own to engage in the formal and informal practices, and then debrief together in the group.

▶ **Engage in insight activities:** Revisit the CBCT for Business and Leadership insight activities, engage in them as a group, and then debrief.

▶ **Engage in formal practices:** Meet to engage in the formal practices as a group.

▶ **Share and apply:** Engage in informal sharing about which CBCT skills and insights have been most meaningful or challenging in work recently.

Mentoring and accountability groups

Working together in pairs or small groups ensures accountability and provides mentoring. Through this work, employees can commit to practices and check in with each other around progress and challenges. They can discuss questions that may arise within this work.

At the start of each month, participants can review the informal practice section of a chosen module and select one or more practices to bring the skills to life. They can then share what they are working on with their accountability partner(s) and agree on next steps.

Certifying Employees in CBCT

As the benefits of CBCT become apparent in the organization, the organization may choose to build internal capacity by certifying employees as CBCT teachers. Providing pathways for employee certification is one of the best and most sustainable ways to ensure supported and ongoing CBCT implementation. The certification process serves to deepen the practice of the participant and increases the organization's capacity to offer and embed CBCT for Business and Leadership into its culture.

Encouraging Employees to Become Certified CBCT Teachers

▶ Offer regular CBCT for Business and Leadership courses. This is a prerequisite for the CBCT Teacher Certification program.

▶ Share the following information about the CBCT Teacher Certification program with employees and leaders interested in the implementation of CBCT for Business and Leadership:

- Opportunities and benefits of certification
  - Ability to teach CBCT to employees and leaders (in their organization and beyond), and to members of the general public
  - Access to a global compassion community of other certified CBCT instructors
  - Deepened familiarity with the content and practices of CBCT and enhanced personal wellbeing
- Funding and scholarship opportunities available (if applicable)
- Certification process details (visit *compassionu.app/teacher-certification* for this information)

 # Integrating into Organizational Structures

Implementing CBCT for Business and Leadership into an organizational culture goes beyond personal and group practice. It also involves integrating the practices and principles into the organization's everyday systems, routines, and structures.

Identify optimal times to integrate key practices and principles of CBCT into routines and structures.

✓ Incorporate CBCT training into an orientation or onboarding session.

✓ Incorporate CBCT settling practices into the start of team meetings, professional development meetings, and conflict mediation meetings.

✓ At the start of a team meeting, provide time to share celebrations, insights, progress, and barriers to the CBCT implementation work.

✓ Apply CBCT principles to the organization's disciplinary policies and/or behavior management approaches. This could include processes that maximize the possibility of:

- Assuring that individual employees are respected for their fundamental desire (and right) to seek wellbeing and avoid distress.

- Staying mindful of the dignity of all individuals—even difficult people and those in difficult circumstances.

- Recalling that all lives have a measure of vulnerability and fallibility, and that no one person or group is free of imperfections.

- Making room for dialogue, mutual understanding, and genuine human connection between all parties.

- When needed, enforcing punitive consequences without shutting off the possibility of genuine remorse, reconciliation, or forgiveness.

✓ Research and choose other wellbeing programs that align with CBCT.

Conclusion

Organizations worldwide are facing a shortage of meaningful relationships, cooperation, and trust in the workplace, undermining optimal conditions for flourishing at all levels. Many are experiencing business trends of poor job satisfaction, a lack of meaning and purpose, and higher burnout among employees and leadership. There are trends of high turnover, low levels of engagement, and increased instances of interpersonal conflicts at work.

Cultivating a culture of compassion is a comprehensive response to this crisis in the workplace. Systematically integrating compassion into organizations promotes psychological safety, purpose, meaningful connections, and resilience, creating a powerful shift toward the greater flourishing and success of individuals, teams, and organizations as a whole.

In this guide, we have outlined a step-by-step process for implementing CBCT for Business and Leadership into an organizational system to foster a sustainable culture of organizational compassion. This process is a realistic approach, based on institutional experiences and best practices within business and leadership, while allowing for individual variation and adaptation. No two organizations are exactly the same, and the way in which CBCT for Business and Leadership is implemented will need to be continuously and creatively considered to encourage each organization's buy-in, commitment, and sustained engagement.

For those who embark on this meaningful journey, know that the Emory Compassion Center will be there to support you, and that there is a growing network of others across the world—educational institutions, corporate organizations, governmental and non-governmental bodies, teachers, researchers, and many others—who are pioneers in the field of compassion. As this network grows, the potential of each individual organization to make a difference will also grow, and each individual voice will be amplified. With sustained effort and mutual support, and with humility and self-compassion, this community will contribute to a more compassionate and ethical world for all.

Keep In Touch

Visit:
compassionu. app/ for-organizations

Email:
partnerships. cbct@emory.edu

Appendix A
Examples of CBCT Journeys

Senior Leader

1 Awareness of CBCT
2 Consideration of strategic alignment
3 Allocation of human and financial resources
4 Receives updates from implementation team regarding pilot (might be part of steering group)
5 Agrees to proceed to post-pilot phase
6 Provides support and visible leadership as needed
7 Includes CBCT updates in internal communications
8 Participates in CBCT training, and more communications

Human Resources / Learning and Development Professional

1 Awareness of CBCT
2 Includes CBCT in L&D planning
3 Training / recruiting CBCT trainers / agree on delivery method (online, in person, hybrid, etc.)
4 Delivers pilot session and measures results
5 Prepares results for senior leadership
6 Delivers wider implementation

New Employee (Starter)

1 Is asked compassion-based questions in interviews
2 Onboarding includes a taster session of CBCT and mentions wider CBCT training
3 Attends CBCT training
4 CBCT cohort stays connected, meets formally and informally to deepen practice
5 Challenging episodes at work are made more manageable through the practice of CBCT

41

Appendix B
Measures

The following is reprinted with permission from Chapter 9 of Kirstie Drummond Papworth's *Compassionate Leadership* (De Gruyter, 2023).

If, then, compassion is an important part of the modern-day organisation, it is important to consider exactly what organisational compassion might be, how to measure and influence it, and how it can be integrated into organisational structures.

An organisation is more than a collection of individuals, albeit ones who typically share a common purpose. Therefore, a compassionate organisation is greater than all the individual propensity for compassion combined. Organisational culture will reflect the prevalent, senior behaviours and leadership's inclination or otherwise towards compassion. Some of this is measurable, yet how people actually feel is also critical to consider.

Have you ever felt happiness? Hopefully. Can you define it? Possibly. Would our definitions of happiness be exactly the same? Unlikely. Although we can all experience something we might call happiness, the term itself may mean different things to different people. The same is true of words such as 'engagement' or 'compassion'. In my own research on AC and OC, the participants were not aware of what the survey was measuring and they may not have been able to define what 'compassion' meant to them. What mattered was the individual experience or perception of compassion; whether they felt heard, seen and supported in times of need. Just like 'happiness' or 'engagement' at work might mean slightly different things depending on our upbringing, life experiences or even first language, it is the experience of compassion that matters more than the precise definition. This is similar to Solomon's concern in his moral psychology essay, discussed earlier in this chapter, where he notes that practical application is more important than precise definitions.

So, similarly to the individual compassion measures in the previous chapter, it is important to keep in mind some health warnings about these organisational compassion measures. Firstly, measures are primarily useful for establishing a benchmark and then assessing subsequent progress. Secondly, the conversations, reflections and actions that these measures prompt are equally, if not more, valuable than any scores they produce. Regardless of the measure used, an organisational compassion score is in itself fairly meaningless. An understanding the reasons for the score matters more, along with tangible actions and genuine commitment to improvement. Thirdly, whilst quantitative scores are useful, qualitative evidence is also worthwhile in order to provide colour and depth to the findings. By and large, the measurement of compassion, whether for ourselves as individuals or for a whole organisation, should be taken as a directional guide rather than a definitive answer.

Part of the reason for noting these provisos is simply that there is no agreed consensus on how to measure the compassion of an organisation. A number of psychology and psychiatry researchers from across the UK and the US completed a meta review of this question (Strauss et al. 2016). They found, unsurprisingly, a lack of consensus on both the definition of compassion and how this should be measured. Nor is there agreement on measuring organisational happiness, wellbeing or even culture, but that does not mean we should not try. Not all that matters can be measured; not all that can be measured matters.

The simplest measure of an organisational outcome is the bottom line. Compassionate leadership affects this too. A Gallup survey (2002) of US employees in the immediate aftermath of the 9/11 attacks asked whether organisations had responded to the attacks in a compassionate way. This included making financial philanthropic donations, giving employees compassionate leave where needed, and addressing employee issues or concerns following the attacks. Where the compassionate response was considered to be excellent, 48% of employees were engaged while only 6% were actively disengaged. By comparison, when the compassionate response was considered to be poor, only 11% were engaged while a staggering 39% were actively disengaged. For comparative purposes in pre-9/11 engagement research, Gallup had found that a 19% active disengagement level was responsible for a loss of around $300 billion in productivity to the US economy. Lack of compassion hurts people and hurts organisations; in Gallup's words, "When compassion is called for, know that your bottom line is at stake."

Key approaches to measuring organisational compassion

There are three main approaches to assessing organisational compassion:

1. Organisational Compassion Quiz

The Compassion Lab at University of Michigan Ross School of Business has partnered with Berkeley's Greater Good Science Center (GGSC) to produce a Compassionate Organisation Quiz. The questions can be easily accessed and tracked via the GGSC website, a link to which is included in the Further Resources section. Questions in this quiz are answered on a 5-point Likert scale, and are predominantly focused on behavioural norms within an organisation, such as: When someone in my organisation expresses that they are having a hard time, most people believe they deserve a caring response.

Or

In my organisation, everyone is too busy to pay attention to whether someone is suffering or not. This quiz is easy to understand, and the GGSC website provides recommendations for action based on the results. As before, the results are useful as a benchmark from which to begin a compassionate journey, and to assess progress.

2. Multiplied Individual Compassion

As organisations are collections of individuals, we can use an individual measure of compassion, such as those outlined in Chapter 8, and create a compassion index by collating all of the responses. This approach is most often used in measuring subjective, largely unquantifiable, yet important concepts such as happiness. The overall compassion trends of an organisation can then be assessed, and action taken to improve the overall trajectory.

Organisational compassion, however, is most likely more than a sum of individual parts. Cultural impacts, professional and personal relational networks, and leadership behaviours all impact organisational systems, so keep this in mind if adopting this approach.

3. Indirect Measures of Compassion

The indirect approach was taken by Ace Simpson and Ben Farr-Wharton (2017) through their assessment of organisational compassion in relation to the more established Perceived Organisational Support (POS), Organizational Citizenship Behaviour (OCB), and employee wellbeing measures. POS assesses the extent to which employees believe that the organisation cares for them and values their contribution, while OCB measures discretionary pro-social employee behaviours. By the same token, measuring Affective Commitment could give an indirect insight into the levels of organisational compassion. Simpson and Farr-Wharton found POS to precede compassion, as well as strong associations between OCB and wellbeing. As a result of their work, they have created the NEAR (Noticing, Empathising, Assessing, Responding) Organisational Compassion Scale.

As with individual measures of compassion outlined in Chapter 8, there is no one size which fits all. Work with what suits your organisation best, adapt question wording to reflect your cultural norms, experiment with nudges and reflect upon your results.

Organisational compassion is a blend of individual perceptions and actions alongside group processes and beliefs, each impacting the other in a constantly adjusting interplay. Developing a compassionate organisation is therefore both art and science, designing supporting structures whilst also enabling flex and adjusting to specific organisational needs. It requires us to simultaneously understand that compassion impacts the bottom line and yet is most usefully measured directionally rather than in absolute terms. The work required to build and maintain such a compassionate organisation is never finished. Stepping back in order to see structural issues, alongside constant upkeep and care, will keep such a compassionate organisation from falling into disrepair. Sustainably compassionate organisations require leaders who reflect on their own intentions, whose multitude of small actions create and maintain psychological safety, and who can handle the 'not knowing' of directional compassionate results.

Such leaders will deliver benefits which will be expressed through the performance results, employee engagement levels and even the survival of their organisations.

Notes

1. Lefebvre, J.-I., Montani, F., & Courcy, F. (2020). Self-compassion and resilience at work: A practice-oriented review. *Advances in Developing Human Resources*, 22(4), 437–452. https://doi.org/10.1177/1523422320949145; Klimecki, O. M., Leiberg, S., Lamm, C., & Singer, T. (2013). Functional neural plasticity and associated changes in positive affect after compassion training. *Cerebral Cortex* 23(7), 1552–1561. https://doi.org/10.1093/cercor/bhs142; Goetz, J. L., Keltner, D., & Simon-Thomas, E. (2010). Compassion: An evolutionary analysis and empirical review. *Psychological Bulletin*, 136(3), 351–374.

2. Pace, T. W. W., Negi, L. T., Adame, D. D., Cole, S. P., Sivilli, T. I., Brown, T. D., Issa, M. J., & Raison, C. L. (2009). Effect of compassion meditation on neuroendocrine, innate immune and behavioral responses to psychosocial stress. *Psychoneuroendocrinology*, 34(1), 87–98. https://doi.org/10.1016/j.psyneuen.2008.08.011; Pace, T., Negi, L., Donaldson-Lavelle, B., Ozawa-de Silva, B., Reddy, S., Cole, S., Craighead, L., & Raison, C. (2012). Cognitively-Based Compassion Training reduces peripheral inflammation in adolescents in foster care with high rates of early life adversity. *BMC Complementary and Alternative Medicine*, 12(Suppl 1), 175. https://doi.org/10.1186%2F1472-6882-12-S1-P175; Pace, T. W. W., Negi, L. T., Dodson-Lavelle, B., Ozawa-de Silva, B., Reddy, S. D., Cole, S. P., Danese, A., Craighead, L. W., & Raison, C. L. (2013). Engagement with Cognitively-Based Compassion Training is associated with reduced salivary C-reactive protein from before to after training in foster care program adolescents. *Psychoneuroendocrinology*, 38(2), 294–299. https://doi.org/10.1016/j.psyneuen.2012.05.019; Reddy, S., Negi, L., Dodson-Lavelle, B., Ozawa-de Silva, B., Pace, T., Cole, S., Raison, C., & Craighead, L. (2013). Cognitive-based compassion training: A promising prevention strategy for at-risk adolescents. *Journal of Child and Family Studies,* 22(2), 219–230. http://dx.doi.org/10.1007/s10826-012-9571-7; Titanji, B. K., Tejani, M., Farber, E. W., Mehta, C. C., Pace, T. W., Meagley, K., Gavegnano, C., Harrison, T., Kokubun, C. W., Negi, S. D., Schinazi, R. F., & Marconi, V. C. (2022). Cognitively Based Compassion Training for HIV immune nonresponders—An attention-placebo randomized controlled trial. *Journal of Acquired Immune Deficiency Syndromes*, 89(3), 340–348. https://doi.org/10.1097/QAI.0000000000002874.

3. Lang, A. J., Casmar, P., Hurst, S., Harrison, T., Golshan, S., Good, R., Essex, M., & Negi, L. (2017). Compassion meditation for veterans with posttraumatic stress disorder (PTSD): A nonrandomized study. *Mindfulness*, 11(1), 63–74. https://doi.org/10.1007/s12671-017-0866-z; Mascaro, J. S., Kelley, S., Darcher, A., Negi, L. T., Worthman, C., Miller, A., & Raison, C. (2016). Meditation buffers medical student compassion from the deleterious effects of depression. *Journal of Positive Psychology*, 13(2), 133–142. https://doi.org/10.1080/17439760.2016.1233348.

4. Mascaro, J. S. et al. (2016).

5. Lang, A. J. et al. (2017).

6. Reddy, S. et al. (2013).

7. Desbordes, G., Negi, L. T., Pace, T. W., Wallace, B. A., Raison, C. L., & Schwartz. E. L. (2012). Effects of mindful-attention and compassion meditation training on amygdala response to emotional stimuli in an ordinary, non-meditative state. *Frontiers in Human Neuroscience*, 6, 292. https://doi.org/10.3389/fnhum.2012.00292; Mascaro, J. S. et al. (2016).

8. Mascaro, J., Rilling, J., Negi, L. T., & Raison, C. (2012). Compassion meditation enhances empathic accuracy and related neural activity. *Social Cognitive and Affective Neuroscience*, 8(1), 48–55. https://doi.org/10.1093/scan/nss095.

9. Gonzalez-Hernandez, E., Romero, R., Campos, D., Burychka, D., Diego-Pedro, R., Baños, R., Negi, L., & Cebolla, A. (2018). Cognitively-Based Compassion Training (CBCT) in breast cancer survivors: A randomized clinical trial study. *Integrative Cancer Therapies*, 17(3), 684–696. https://doi.org/10.1177/1534735418772095; Sun, S., Pickover, A. M., Goldberg, S. B., Bhimji, J., Nguyen, J. K., Evans, A. E., Patterson, B., & Kaslow, N. J. (2019). For whom does Cognitively Based Compassion Training (CBCT) work? An analysis of predictors and moderators among African American suicide attempters. *Mindfulness*, 10(11), 2327–2340. https:// doi.org/10.1007/s12671-019-01207-6; Titanji, B. K. et al., (2022).

10. The World Health Organization. (2024, September 2). Mental health at work. https://www.who.int/news-room/fact-sheets/detail/mental-health-at-work

11. Akgün, A. E., Keskin, H., & Etlioğlu Başaran, H. T. (2025). Organizational compassion: A conceptual extension and scale development. *Current Psychology*, 44(5), 3787–3810. https://doi.org/10.1007/s12144-025-07442-6